THE NEXT LEVEL OF KNOWLEDGE

<u>DISCLAIMER</u>

This book contains solution to the impediment of general commotion of human. It has deliberately given its own way of perceiving the human nature and their way of body and mind workings. Do not trust the book if you feel yourself that it has no possibilities of being such. Trust it when it really has some usefulness on your life. Also, is to have knowledge of this divinity is a good in itself even if you don't use any method written below. This book is not created to harm any of the people, society or ethnicity. Its motive solemnly and confined towards individual perception of the writer and bound to the perception of a person. There is no obligation or enforcement towards what it has been written. Deny the book thoughts if you don't want to hear about humans and their minds workings.

TABLE OF CONTENT:

CHAPTERS:

1. PERCEPTION AND PSYCHOLOGY

2. LIE

3. KNOWLEDGE AND WISDOM

4. DOMINATION

CHAPTER 1:   PERCEPTION and PSYCHOLOGY:

When it comes to the perception, every human is different. We love to hear the perception and thinking towards over something; over and under some circumstances of someone. Whatever we hear, see them doing the thing, that's somehow it was programmed on their mind.

Let's have some questions; how the mind is programmed even all of us are unique and different somehow?!!

HOW??

Some basic (internal) elements of human behaviour we must know before entering into the deep subject:

- Love, hate, anger, happiness, sadness, kindness, selfishness, desire etc. (backed up feelings by human body)
- Pain, torture and tension
- Sex, age
- knowledge

These are the basics of human behaviour where the perception starts or fluctuates.

The external factors that determine our behaviour and thinking:

- Family, society where we are born.

- Culture and religion also affect how we feel and think about something.
- Obligations and time.

All the normal humans: I am talking about the normal humans and their way of thinking falls; under these internal and external categories no matter how hard you try to find the differentiation it will come under it.

One another factual fact about humans in this world is; not even a single of them will have a second thought of; as if they are the inferior, they always think that they are superior, let me give it a precise meaning by giving a sentence "yes! This is what I am.!!", if they were succeeded. Even a seven-bottle drinker have a will to drink to the eight one, despite the thing, he is not in the condition to drink, however a sheer will to drink.

Why we give priority to Face?

Because your face tells everything, not only your identity but also all the emotions are confronted by your face. Your age can be determined just by looking at the charm of your face. It's just we came up with slight mistake that some unique people who have a naturally given face that we can't follow their emotion through their face, otherwise 99 out of 100 we do, and we can. Just we must focus on them and buy some moment for them to show up.

Characteristics of Perception and Psychology:

I have given the introductory part of the perception and psychology where the human natures are beginning with and the prior influences helps developing the perception and psychology. The main achievement on psychology is to perceive the target or subject behaviour, habits and other terminology which he exercises, or haves or haves not. The person desire is another crucial factor that must be included while studying the psychological manner of the people or subject. So, the determinants need to be categorised to make a good follow up while on going with the proceeding of any study or work.

Characteristics of Perception:

- Analysis and thinking are based on time lapse (how much he lived) and experience,

- The haves or haves not also make huge differences on someone's perception,

- Desire (willingness, ability, backup) also makes differences on the perception of the people,

- Norms and values, culture and religions help ignite of certain way of thinking as they are based on the same manual input of regulation in regard to such field or values,

- Perception is lacked or few if someone doesn't have much access to the all available resources, (eg: a born baby left for five years without hearing a human voice or any sound),

- An unawakened wisdom on human can never feel that his/her perception are driven by the externalism and manual input.

Characteristics of Psychology:

- Behaviour is based on people thought process, perception and reflexes what they keep doing or keep thinking,

- Study always should have a base, how a subject is driven or has influences with,

- Prediction and accuracy on it will be positive if the base elements are well studied on human or subject,

- The occurrence and repetition are to be taken as crucial information for the prediction.
- The irrational decision making may incorrect the outcome of prediction (Subject or target).

Chapter 2: LIE

Is the cover everyone had on their face, through mouth, through emotion, everyone today here is lying.

Let's talk about the tactic how to catch people who are lying?

Many experiments have towed the clue how to catch up the lie, many machines have been made to know who are lying. However, there are some way people lie and we can catch them while they are lying on something because we don't have the machine with us all the time.

How we catch them?

"Frequency" is one absolute method how we can deal with the lies. How much frequently people are lying? Another is "case sensitive" lie which is often found on those cases where the matters are most secret, and they are qualitative, highly preserved by someone on some circumstances of use. It depends on how much they value those things to come up with different lies.

Most of the people who are lying does have no guilt on them that they lie. Some people have their uncommon thinking on lies. Some people can't stand with lies.

So, as a whole; lies can be detected on:

- How much people is a frequent liar?
- Materiality involved in lies,
- Feelings involved to keep it secret,

- Fraudulent activities involved.
- Lie for happiness
- Master liar
- Lie as a hiding place or corner/ PROFESSIONAL LIES
- DREAM.

Gestures shown by the people who lie:

- People seems quite "**confident**" what they are telling, there is a lie hidden (**frequent liar**). The confident on them is only backed up with lie, it can be detected if you cross check them with other relative few questions and suddenly they will start with **anger** and **irritation**.

- When materiality is involved in lying, people who are trying to obtain them with lie seems **confident** and people who refuse to lose them will lie and are in **tension**.

- **Straight answers** are given, and **repetitive straight answers** are delivered by the people who lies on material things or informative secrets which are not allowed for spell. Here, the talkative capacity of the person is biased by the superior involvement to make them lie or forged not to talk.

- Fraudulent activities should be covered with lies; this is how one thinks when the activities are done. It's not necessary that it must have to be covered with lies.

- Master liar often found in politician, leadership and management who have the major authorities not to make material misstatement however they do and cover with the lies. Some mysteries were never sort out when it comes to the politician affairs and issues.

- Lies are often put to use as a mask to cover the face of reality, pain inside, smile outside; where smile is a lie.

- DREAM: how many people think the dream as a contingent lie with your own self until it is fulfilled. Sometimes your dream could go wrong, we are lying to our self; aren't we? I prefer it as a contingent lie with some probability which may occur or may not. However, dream is a good thing which possess happiness and misery.

Be aware of some people who have following character:

I am not talking about the abnormal people. Normal people also have different character on them.

- **Silent people**: They are gullible, over thinkers, sometimes driven by negativity. This character has either high level of positiveness or high level of restiveness on them. So, it depends from which quality they are driven. I am not saying them bad however; on which quality they are driven.

- **Mediator**: This character can cause you either high profit or loss to you with his informative power as a mediator. They are boon at the other hand can cause huge damage to you depending on them. Try to avoid bias with people of this character and acknowledge them well so they feel appreciated and don't let them feel that your appreciation is unnatural.

- **Politician**: Some people are politicians by their working field however some people are naturally politician from their mindset. They can affect your single bread if they possessively want to make things on such.

Even you may fall on this category: to whom they are reading now; my opinion to them as common, you guys are best, you are doing super, use your capacity to build the next generation to deliver the best out of the best to this world. This world has so many eras to pass.

- **Immediate reactor:** Their decision fluctuates as they have less tolerance level. People like them are always empty handed.

- **Talkative person who always have secret**: Secrecy is a good thing. But you can't trust to those who have secrets. Never trust people who have secrets. Don't avoid them however create a mindset for them as a suspect until they reveal the secrets. Disclosure is the only way to make trust.

Test by yourself, observing the targeted person under the circumstances given by this book. As a whole, you may find the differences on the prediction of yours if the following people are observed by you:

- Lunatic
- Personality Disorder
- Crazy
- People who have already read this book and already knew that you are observing them.

Other than them, it won't make such differences on your prediction and to understand them. You will not fail yourself from misleading character which you can't understand or handle them. Be Your Own Boss. Observing the background of internal and external as well as the fact about past, their economy and mindset flow; you will be able to predict how they are going to react in the next situation. This is why the past records are withheld by the human Resource management of an organisation with disclosing perquisites requirement data known as name, address, birth, family, crime check, education, experience, etc.

One last thing about lies is they are either used by the strongest or by the weakest because it helps the strongest to possess its thrown and the weakest (I am not saying poor), the weakest because he always tried to become clever and strong. People often feel that telling lies or keeping secrets makes then stronger and clever. Disclosures of certain circumstances is prohibited doesn't mean that we have to lie in each case. There are certain ways to deal with it. Please deal with it without lying it. You will find the differences.

CHAPTER 3: KNOWLEDGE and WISDOM:

Hello there, this chapter discuss about knowledge and the background of knowledge where they are coming from. What type knowledge people possess? Who are projecting this knowledge? How this knowledge is affecting us?

Definition of Knowledge: This is a required, multi-dimensional, cognitive, persuasive, qualifiable, builder of capacity and dignity of wisdom on one human. It's a never-ending process. We all know that knowledge is gathered in memory power of human mind;

internal and external like memory other than human. Internal memory is inside the human and external memory is outside memory form invented by the human for persuasive purpose and backup system. Memory is just a vacant space where you can record something or some information. Memory and knowledge are different like water (knowledge) and pot (memory). Same thing goes with your brain as well.

Thought Process: This process is reticulated by the five sense organs and are backed up by the feelings and emotions one had, or those feelings and emotions exaggerated from the potential sensation. A thought process may be same on every human which rely on (auto generated) by the human ness however it is critically influenced by the manual way of thinking as there are some put to use emotion on certain circumstances.

We involve the brain as the solemn part of thought process. However, the five senses are continuously feeding the brain for the thought process. Whatever we think is the part of internalise and external feed gained from the five senses. Moreover, the internal points from the body root to the body top of the spinal cord also holds the memory and information which works as the information feed to the brain. One of the examples of the information feed from the spinal cord to the brain is the reflexes and the stimuli (first performed then informed to the brain).

Automated (Natural) way of thinking and reaction(stimuli): This contains anger, tear, fear, kindness, love and affection. These are also known as the base of the emotion which has major impact on how you think after such feelings. They are auto generated from the true self. I am not putting any scientific figures and research outcomes which has already been done before this book because they can be found easily in google. So, in the matter of persuasion, the base of these emotions is auto generated from the natural perception of a human nature.

Manual (input) Way of thinking: These thoughts are manual, societal, environmental driven; what we learnt from the society, input knowledge from the government content of discrepancies on schools and colleges and the reaction of others made us to think in certain ways. In other words, these are the way of thinking which we are allowing ourselves to act in that way to adapt with the environment.

A knowledge is known as the manual input which we gain from this world from copying and learning. If we found something new which nobody has found yet is known as our discovery. The so-called invention is known as the discovery which was new to the human world.

Apart from the definition of the Manual Input of knowledge, there is something else that I want to say; is the manipulation and effect of the manual input which has had on human in positive and negative manner. The human him/herself always serve as a vacant memory on which there need to put some input to grow up with this current dynamism. In disguise, the fresh human which has no experience at all can be easily manipulated by the effect of false education and wrong preaching and teaching. On the contrary, human can become as the top personality by the manual input of knowledge from the perspective of positive education and teachings. How many of us feel that whatever we learnt from the early child was helpful?

Most of us. Meanwhile, how many of us feel that something at sometimes that we read or learnt was incorrect? These sorts of feeling only raised in our thought when we are experienced enough to know what is wrong and what is right?!!!

A manual knowledge can be boon or sin as the user passes it to the next generation for how he wants to!! For an instance, when a manual input for feelings is changed for like, umm......!! we have to laugh when a person dies. This input may be weird however, people may react the same if their manual knowledge has been concreted through that way. So, this is a serious thing that a person can be manipulated by the way of manual input knowledge to reticulate the thinking of a person. The current dynamics of knowledge is only limited to the manual input of knowledge. People are digging more into it through research and planning. Furthermore, with use of manual input knowledge people can grasp the techniques and make up to experience. Here, the manual input knowledge is mixed with the trainings and time lapse to give out the name called experience. What is experience? How do we define the experience and how our body signifies the experience? These two questions are from two separate perspective in my acknowledgement. I would define the experience as the practical process and trainings backed up with the lapse of time along you live with that knowledge and practice with due care at that certain period. However, how your body identify that knowledge and those practice is similar another thing which human are grasping as experience. As the time lapse, with certain physical practice, the body stimuli and subconsciousness, start to workout with that practices, it mixes those practices with body stimuli and will perform the same and these makes a habit to the physical body.

Now, these practices which are a mix up with the stimuli are just acting like the natural stimuli. On the consequences, they are manual stimuli which will go blunt as the body doesn't practice with the same. But natural stimuli are those reactions which the body never forget on its own. Its incapability due to the cause of ageing or paralyses may be the different circumstances. Here, memory for the manual input knowledge works as a crucial factor. You may be wondering if the manual input knowledge has existence, then why not the automated knowledge? Where is our Automated knowledge? Those grasps are just the world's manual input. From where we would get this Automated knowledge? From the reflexes or from the thinking? No, No, No!!! Its hidden somewhere within us, we have to unwrap the knowledge package which is inside of us. But, how? We are cellular organism. Each cell of our body contains memory. Not only the brain, whole body has its own memory system with an expiration period. You can train your mind through manual input knowledge likewise the same could be done with the whole cellular organ and whole body. The optimism of the body hasn't yet yield from the current human side. May be, we don't know as well till now because no one has taught us how to. We are only relying all the time same with the manual input knowledge. Let's not talk here about the automated knowledge. I will go further on last episode of this book about this main theme which I am trying to employ from this book to the whole world.

Link of automated and the manual imputes of Knowledge: the automated knowledges are the fresh creativeness which holds the key to move the person from the direction of the stone age to this vast human development. The manual imputes of knowledge are the record of those creativeness invented and sought from the automated knowledge. Suitable examples of the automated knowledge which has gained its nature into the form of manual imputes are the languages, writing words, the 24 hours calculation of the day in the number of clockwise, the generic rules, etc. it was first sought by the illiterate but very intelligent ancestors who developed those general terms and now has become the manual imputes which cannot be broken or elsewise changed and are ready made knowledge to us. So, the record keeping in the milestones, papers and nowadays in the software has made the manual imputes of knowledge very strong as it serves as the evidence of its existence in some physical or in software content. That's why people are more relying on those knowledges which are a readymade imputes, which gives a ton of feed to the brain.

Your brain works few times more if it must give some unidentified problems needs to be solved when there are no materials available as references. At the other hand, if you keep yourself updated with the material references you will never use your brain as the first immediate solver despite indulging yourself in somehow in the references.

When reasoning of your own becomes lower, the sharpness of you tempt to be degraded and keep at its inferior. The character of using other materials has ethics of becoming right rather than using own brain and "motives of brain".

"Motives of Brain" - the existence of the brain and neurons on your body has some motive to perform on their own and its seizure to perform some exercise will have the effect to become a lower server; meaning it will go drain and can't keep to have its own base. Those mind or brain which motive has already been disturbed by the excessive use of manual imputes might suffer from the depression and other anxiety. Those brain will have suffered and in-trauma of keep suffering, and fear of getting lost or being alone. So, meaningful way of getting these, your mind needs an exercise either way a difficult situation with no references or support or with peaceful enact to ease your brain to find its neutrality.

Wisdom: The state of being freed from any dependency like knowledge, physical state and free of fear from any contingencies is known as wisdom. The definition may vary relating the person involved in different sectors and their way of understanding. The word "wisdom" solemnly contains the power of decision making on one hand. All of these were generic term of "wisdom". Now, according to my opinion to the word "wisdom"; when a person obtains the Automated input of Knowledge or found the source of automated knowledge which lies within us then the person deemed to have got his/her wisdom. He/she can cherish his/her personal decision-making process and can positively affect the mass in general.

Definition of Automated Knowledge: the word "automated knowledge" serves as the knowledge which has a base within us but no medium where it is coming from. You may not be able to sense the medium from where it is coming however you will be able to sense it as it is playing inside us and healthily helping us in a Bonafede manner with 100% of accuracy on the outcome of the source information implication. The instinct and hunch are the very puny level of automated knowledge which I am referring as an example of it. The brain (mind) produce this type of knowledge.

Dependency on Hunch and Instinct: I would rather say, in practice; we do not believe and depend on the hunch because we need proof and existence on the subject matter so discussed. Nobody can give you certain proof on their guess. Forecasting something is on the different criteria. Estimation has its own base trend and expected percentage output. What I am trying to relate on these descriptions is hunch and instinct has no value in front of those expectation made so forth from the base value and knowledge of trend. But still, hunch and instinct have some influence reacting upon those knowledges of expectation in general. We mere humans, can't throw it away coz it lies in our subconscious.

How we can figure out the Automated Knowledge?

Automated knowledge is produced knowledge from your mindset, heart set, body set, from the all of yourself within you. Your one single cell can generate this knowledge. It is unusual, gathered from the energy what we have. Sources of energy that our human body is consuming may be food, water. However, let's go a little deep about how many types of energy we consume?

Sources of Energy:

Food, water and air are those instant energy to be taken by the human. Out of these, two of them seems manual whereas one seems automatic. Respiration is automated, we need air as a source of life input. Food and water give chemical and mineral energy.

One another form of energy we are taking but we may not be able to carve it until we have some evidence on it; is cosmic energy. This energy we are taking is while we are under sleeping mode. Our body is functioning like the battery mode when in sleep. What a drag?

Who told you? How do you know? Well, I didn't even know it until some other people let me know it. My **GURU MR. GANESH KARKI** while in the study of meditation led me the knowledge of this energy to feel it. Well, I am not guru so I may not be able to give you that feelings of energy however to those who profounder themselves as gurus and established in a legal way to do meditation will or can help you to feel that energy. For Sure!! Stop yourself being amazed and join the classes. Oh!! I think I am going slight outwards the topic. Pinpointing the matter about the energy we grab from cosmic; hey, are you with me!!?? Ok, lets conclude the energy explanation. There are three sources of energy, they are:

- *Breathing (Automatic input)*
- *Cosmic energy (Automatic input)*
- *Food and Water (manual input)*

As above shown, the automated input and the manual input has some relevance to the depth of the knowledge. Ok!! What was the topic we were on? Automated Knowledge to be figured out!!!!! How? Simply put, the better and healthier food and fresh water we consume, the stronger and the healthier we become, that's correct!! On the other hand, oxygen and its mixture have direct relation with the living of every living creature. Does oxygen give us power, no!!! and yes!!! it's a source of living. But if we focus a little more on breathing, another Automatic input can be in our grasp that is cosmic energy. So, these automatic inputs will give out the automated knowledge. Air is also a form of energy, have you ever heard the air makes you stronger and healthier. Yes, to healthier and stronger, but at the same time we need food and water input to maintain our body. So, could we have some probability to say that the air component has more to give in our lives. Air also gives more than a healthy, simply it gives knowledge that's it. Logic is that it is one of the oldest elements which has been giving life from evolution to till date. Question arises the element which gives us life; isn't the source has its own living form? Answer can't be proven through the science however mythologically, it is as good as living creature. So, it contains all the memory back from all living and non-living existed from the evolution and it works as the information base for the automated knowledge input. Concluding the point, what we must find out is through meditation. Cosmic energy, oh!! Another automated input source of energy, this contains, huge knowledge source, feelings capsize, accuracy of your thinking determined by this input. Grab it as more as you can. Both, the automated inputs are eyeless driven, only sense can work on them.

Assumptions and decisions:

- *A brain in neutrality never takes a wrong decision. So lucky you, because you are always right when you take decision being neutral. The capacity of the brain to decide doesn't comply the total decision making by the brain itself. Your level of energy also determines the capacity to make decision on it. Just like, the various stronger countries showing their interest and domicile accounting to their level of energy; the same our mind perform at the different level of energy to make its decision. So, to make a very good and precise decision, the neutrality of your mind and the level of energy on your total body should be either correctly rectified or make it into the normal position.*

How the mind take assumption now is something external and internal. The external environment that will level up your stigma and potential pre makes of copied knowledge and the basis of it, or the internal environment is the inner neutral point and the amount of energy that you possess on yourself.

The so-called copy pasted knowledge has readymade assumption to spoke with. You need not need to make any changes on that economic point. This point is economic because you don't have to waste any second of time to make the assumption on behalf of something. Those things are already made assumption which are copy pasted as general knowledge from the manual basis of input.

The manual input has something already skewed on your mind to make any assumption. This is the part where you could be wrong. The wrong amidst where your mind is drowning is because of the manual basis assumption which you have taken. Not necessarily, all the manual basis assumptions should be wrong however the maximum chances when people are getting into the wrong decision is because of the dependent on assumption on manual basis of imputes of knowledge.

How are manual imputing assumption related?

Your basis of knowledge imputes has series of condition how it was imputed in. The mind reflexes those condition in a random series of decision making. It takes those assumptions as base and rely on them as if you believe in them truly and enthusiastically. The decision then has two streams of being right or wrong on the given circumstances. The double assumption on after the outcome of decision that you are still right even if the outcome is wrong makes another barrier to put to use that you were right, but these circumstances proves you wrong. The anti-alliance of being wrong may be truly right but the mind assumption doesn't let you see those unwrapped right being a barrier to the mind. This is how it works when you put to use the manual input of knowledge to make a decision.

How are Automated imputes assumptions are more accurate?

Imputes with sudden reaction

This assumption has its no certainty how it relies on the base queries. The queries or problem has its own criteria and automated knowledge is silent when you are confronting the problems. Let the flow of problems be untouched and undisturbed because the more you disturb the problem the more severe impact it has on you. In the midst of silence if there comes a solution out of nowhere but in your mind, this means your automated imputes has aroused. If not, you are not been able to ignite the power of automated knowledge. :

The base of your knowledge has another dimension to rely on it. This is the truly your decision beside your knowledge limitation to certainty. This knowledge has a ignite power to build you strong and capable to grow you through the situation led by the life. These imputes are self-grown from your mind, besides your thinking something comes automatic like you are working in a kitchen, you are so busy and quite helping yourself hardly to make your dish taste good, at a point you stopped, that moment you got some idea on other matter which you were not thinking. Anything but not the dish and cookery. Maybe you have got an idea of the key relation of market strategy of your upcoming business.

Imputes with serial reaction:

This is a problem-solving method that your mind triggers itself when you try it to make it calmer and subject to neutrality. The neutrality possesses some inertia of rest which will lead to right decision-making capabilities of your mind. Most of the people have recognised this method or technique as it has already happened to you lots of time, but you can't address it more precisely. So how this imputes has a serial reaction on them?!! Put your mind on hold for a time being and take your problem on your mind on a series, to say make your problem a series. Review it and stay calm, stay calm for a bit and think nothing, after a moment your mind will solve that problem with different option, say it with two option; if this this thing happens this will seize to remain. On the other hand, if this thing is not about to happen the following may not seize. Then you will prepare for both of it happening and non-happening of the both criteria. While being prepared for the both options you will have more confident and set level of energy to deal with both kind of circumstances, you will not be doomed, and you will not fall down. This is the path of serial reaction of automated knowledge which may not lead you to win but to keep you on in the line. Win situations are followed by the sudden reaction of automated knowledge when you are in the edge of corner to lose or fall behind or something when you have no capabilities to keep up, these sudden automated imputes will help you to save yourself by giving you a lending hand of win. Trust me if some brains have capabilities to grab energy from all sides, it does possess these powers to help you on your scarce.

How Does automated knowledge works on you?

Even if you ask, I can't be able to give you evidence on these sorts of Knowledge working on the circumstances, or may fail while providing the evidence because this knowledge is not in your hand, when it comes it comes like a flash back, highly infusing and giving you the optimum judgement capacity to work with your right and wrong 'decision besides your logic and beyond your science capacity. When it comes, you will feel like all these information's are not in the base of your mind, never heard of it, never seen of it, never smelt, out of your five senses but still there is another base of knowledge which just help you to make a precise decision. This base of knowledge is not manual so that's why I put a category, Automated Knowledge or Automated base of Knowledge.

Now, let's talk about the "knowledge sources base" on your mind, they are Manual base input, experience stimuli and age (time lapse). So, these are the main sources of input on our mind and body system. (Body System knowledge) a physical experience helps body to contain those moves and reflexes and mix up with its stimuli, it is also known as the knowledge of our body system. Whatever you decide and act against and along the circumstances are driven from the knowledge gain from the above state. On the contrary, there comes the "automated knowledge input", which are driven from some energy based and will provide you the 100% accuracy on what you are doing.

For an instance; I don't hesitate to say this, but this happened to me once in a lifetime that I was able to pull out the automated source of knowledge from the inside of my energy tabulated on me. That was the time when me and my friend gone to ride a motorcycle with no helmet and licence, we were young and stupid and whatever we did was stupidly wrong that time which I realised after some lapse of time. We were caught by the traffic police and suddenly stuck in the issues of the traffic police rules violation. We didn't have any evidence of the ownership of that bike was ours and felt that we will lose the bike for sure in the hand of government scrap. It was my fathers' bike, Dipesh was riding it and he was so upset its because of him we were caught by the police. Stupid me, I was so compelled from my true self and happened to have a certain kind of feeling that we have to get that bike whatsoever. We Sat aside the corridor watching the traffic police doing their job. Suddenly, some tickles inside me began and was talking to me, there were five traffic polices, all at once it was saying that this policeman will go after another chasing, another will turn back around, one police officer is willingly to offer you let go the bike because our bike was so old and the ownership paper was as good as lost, two other policeman will be busy doing their own stuff, you have to ask Dipesh to go aside of the turning point first, you should go get a bike and RUN.......!!!!!! What??? Who was that???? I was stiffened but I knew what will happen to the next few minutes already, then I copy pasted the same conversation to Dipesh. I asked him to go for sure on the turning point before I grab the bike. I also told him the conversation of those policeman what will they be doing in the next minute. I did explain, please trust me, he didn't trust me, neither Do You? But of course, he obeyed me, He was running to the next edge of the turning point, I grabbed the bike gave a good nice start kick on the manuals; oh! it does start man!!! I was a goner. Later that time, Dipesh was astonished.

Chapter 4: Domination:

Does knowledge have a power of Domination? Is nation being powerful by the help of knowledge? What is the dominating part of the world? If Knowledge was there, are everybody getting the wisdom and freedom? Is development a cause of knowledge?

Knowledge never dominates any of the personalities; yes, it is partially true that the knowledge helps in the phase of the development **however** the domination is caused by the other factor's relation with the humankind. Knowledge and wisdom are different parts which can be used for the domination. But what is that the dominating circumstances existed in the world from the very beginning to till now? The answer is the use of energy and resources and the accumulation of the energy for a time being. The use of energy and how to meld the energy could be the part of the knowledge but directly knowledge don't serve as the purpose of the domination. So, developed personalities or nation has direct relation with the energy and resources to dominate and been using the knowledge as the partial control of it. So, you must be cautious with them who possess the power of utility and power of energy. For an instance, you have a chance of less possibilities of threat in consult with the lecturer than the wrestler who has high temper. Here, the temper is in all being as the embodied nature, the meaningful example is to create a sample to provide the differences between the two personalities who has the knowledge and on the other hand has the energy on him for a time being. Here, the first has the personalities to avoid fight because of his lifestyle that he has to maintain his profession without a fight and keeps his desire lower in dispute. The later has the first priority to be involved into the fight and his reflexes keep him high and ready to battle. The key is first the emotion and the element to abate the emotion is the environment where they and their personalities are growing together. Is to become knowledgeably dominant is other thing; has its own pros and cons to deal with the environment. Wherever the debate arises, there will be the dispute among the knowledge and the energy. Those who have knowledge may find themselves to work in the peaceful way or may with tricky manner however energy works as its rest or in motion. The scientific definition of inertia of rest and motion has given the exact definition of the energy and its state of being rest or motion. Now, what I meant to say is that the domination is the cause of desire proacting from the environmental and inner influences and character that one man has within himself. Taking as the earth division with the parts as a nation being developed and powerful in themselves in possession of the energy and resources with them. Not every people of the country has possessed by the utter knowledge and wisdom contrarily can have used them as the resources to manipulate other economic resources in the form of labour. Money has also worked as the same as a means to deliver yourself a power. Is money a crude knowledge? No, its not. Of Course, it isn't because the money never served as a k knowledge but instead its mere definition as the purchasing power of the resources has termed itself as another form of energy in it. Well, money has the power of artificial energy which has the dominant role to play as the greatest means to manipulate, uses, restrict, everything like a knowledge, resources, energy and someone's emotion as well. The next generation is being highly influenced by the ruckus of money as its premium importance consequences the human nature and happiness to be realised only if one possesses money. It has already become inevitable, indispensable for one to live as a happy life. The uneven disasters and calamities are some examples; when the occur, the value of money will disappear for a time being. The system of earth nowadays isn't working with the elements which has provided us life, like the sunlight, the air, the land, instead the money to buy them or their next form (human perspective). We, the humans, in the meantime are attractive with the energy. Say it or not, we need energy to live as base, to enjoy as mid, to dominate as uppercut. So, everybody in this world is influenced by the energy either its natural form or the artificial form. We bow to the god because of his energy, not ours. So, everything here is depend upon energy simple and direct logic.

To be continued..........